One life
One Journey

Gary George

This short book is related with my spiritual beliefs and does not impose or reflect on any psychological or scientific understanding. Observations of current social trends in parenting and our social skills within society have brought about the writing of this book.
How we interact with our children, family & friends using words and body language creating awareness on how we currently reflect our materialistic views and distort our children's beliefs.

www.garygeorgeauthor.com

DEDICATION

To my beautiful wife Carol, who understands &
supports me in every aspect of life, and allows
myself to dream big and create new realities.

ACKNOWLEDGMENTS

I would like to acknowledge my parents who have
long passed. Their zest & enjoyment of life, gave
myself a great appreciation of everyday journeys.
A lifetime filled with laughter & joy.

CONTENTS

INTRODUCTION

"Mystical Words" Our children in their first steps for life's journey the universal code empowering wonderment, achievement and understanding. Actions we present to our children today good or indifferent brand your children's values and achievements throughout their life's journey.

Written words seize the imagination; practise and disciplines ignite the amazement of twenty five "Mystical Words" to authenticate and sometimes question our influence on our own children is an astonishing power. It is a gift that has been passed on with every previous generation, but how do we know if our perceptions and beliefs compel the right path for our children? The honest answer is we don't.

Do twenty five mystical words acknowledge their journey and embellish yours, to sit and read with your child the wonderment of an uncomplicated universal language that every nationality understands and acknowledges, even if words aren't spoken?

Writing this book was about my connection with the universe. These words resonate for the now and the future, learn from the past but live for today and tomorrow. This understanding is a measurement of me, living in harmony with our surrounds and the society we are connected with. Open up your heart and mind to the universe and the universe reveals an extraordinary you!

Learning with our children today unlocks your insight for their potential future & yours.

Life is a journey! To take the first steps in a simple formula but a lifetime of beautiful practice. To be a better person and hold true to these twenty five virtues.

Your undertaking, today, is to sign and date the contract to yourself and your children, to start your Journey in the "now" to revisit this path you have started and reflect on your progress for the future. Ask yourself this? Do I view the world through my child's eyes? Do my steps prepare my children for the better; are my words intuitive with virtues or caustic by choice?

Take this moment to reflect a better you..............

Date _____

Parent's Name _____

Sign _____

Child's Name _____

Sign _____

TRUTH 1

"Truth" is the value of *"truth"* commanding and potent, pure in essence? It has no explanation, but it exists. It is locked into our subconscious, our soul and being. It is a primordial. This word narrates our body language; communication skills & behaviour "Its" affects are beautiful or soul destroying if miss used at the same time.

Without *"Truth"* should our memories exist? Without *"Truth"* creating and preserving the "now" or a future is it possible?

"Truth" is not subjective, never judges or rationalises. Truth is factual, or your perceptions of truth are factual. No two persons have the same memory and have caused conflict and splendour inherently throughout our history. Truth has a future as it relates to the now. For every word that is spoken today, the potency of this value causes a response from the future and creates a memory for the past. In the future *"Truth"* evaluates our reasoning and shifts our subconscious to make changes to the way we converse with others or to hide the truth!

Throughout our tarnished history hidden *"truths"* has been responsible and created more conflict and wars. If the truth is pure by virtue then hidden truths create polar opposites. Should hidden truths be the devil in disguise? I'm not a religious person, but I comprehend the unruly destructive force of hidden truths.

From the birth, a child is seeking the truth. The moment their eyes open to the wonderment that surrounds them, gaining familiarity with every aspect of life. At first your little person cannot tell you this, but as time passes does your persona impinge on their decision to speak their first word. Mum, Dad or a swear word?

How many times have you heard this story? Do parents and family infuse perceptions or imperfect memories on children thus creating a negative impact? Remember when your children arrive at the world is their dependence reliant on you? Are children born with opinions, perceptions, language, motor skills or does this little person learn these skills from their parents? As parents consider for a moment….. What spoken words are interpreted by your children? Reflect the *"Truth"* for a moment……

A simple analogy is racism! Is your child born a racist? I should say no. Is it the "Truth" or an understanding your child has heard or maybe parents passing on points of view?

All children are born pure of heart. Their dreams have no boundaries your children see no indifferent colours! Why do we not all get along with diversified cultures of the world? If we were brought up with "truths" and not points of view, should our universe change for the better?

"Truth" creates a harmonious life to engage our children's future. Many analogies and different situations prevent *"Truths"*

As parents should we say this is all too hard, is this truth? Or maybe as parents we should say this should be done, let's make changes! Make a better universe in which to live? Now you understand why the word "Truth" is extraordinarily potent, a virtue that should never be miss-used in any language. As a parent, should we try to encourage & influence a child's *"Truth"*? Encourage your children to create their own learning levels & beliefs and not ours.

Disciplines and learning to break a lifetime of bad habits are sometimes overwhelming but isn't your child worth the excitement when you do? Just maybe your child just wants to learn the *"Truth"*

≈Truth pure in nature

FORGIVENESS 2

"Forgiveness" touches our soul with kindness a heavenly virtue, removing the heavy burdens of guilt. It takes a universal power to forgive but rewards are a plenty once you have achieved this level of consciousness. When you forgive a person entirely, you no longer feel the slightest bit of resentment against them. Heavy burdens influence our health and mental well-being it keeps a person locked with insecurities and removes self confidence to progress with their conscious life and holds us back for enjoying and creating new memories in the now and future.

As you mature in life, your connections with society grow, you meet individuals that give clear indications their lives are locked in a past memory and cannot move on with their future or for that matter live in the now. Giving clear messages of previous times, holding onto the memories of good experiences up until that event or continually bringing up the event in the conversation. Generally the experience is with someone or something where their feelings have been treated fairly unjustly or a traumatic event. Perceptions of an incident as discussed in truths have caused great conflicts and burdens with no two memories concluding an exacting memory.

Within a micro second of an incident, the soul has been hurt, burdened with profound judgement and until the learning of forgiveness begins your soul remains locked subconsciously. Taking on the event as a learning process and not a universal judgement releases the understanding of forgiveness, your journey to create.

Perceptions for a child are somewhat fragile and easily bruised. When we are young and learning boundaries, our innocence takes words to heart even if the child is in the wrong. Gentle dealings with these indiscretions assist in our child's learning and development. After an incident and once a child has been reassured with love, speaking with "truths" and making them aware of consequences for their actions and explaining their behaviour, the "forgiveness" process has begun. With every learning aspect good or indifferent children recognise the respect and love you have for them, making every indiscretion a learning of "boundaries" and not a burden placed on the soul.

As incidents come up in our lives, traumatic events we usually have no control over, our subconscious analysis's this event a thousand times over in our head no matter what age we are.

Two things tend to happen at this stage, as time progresses you carry this burden with you for an extremely long time and sometimes forever or you learn to forgive, acknowledging the wrong and make this incident an incident of growth but it takes great courage, fortitude & discipline to do this.

"Forgiveness" understands, acknowledges the wrong or our faults, asking for forgiveness when we have done wrong brings society closer. Family, partners, friends and strangers are aware that you have a higher awareness and understanding of morality. Learn from negative events and emotions. Acknowledging the wrong liberates your soul.

≈Truth initiates Forgiveness

LOVE 3

"Love" is everything. True love has no boundaries it surpasses our physical realms. Love is limitless; no scale has measured "its" beauty, strength, passion and wonderment for a loved one, a blending of emotions for our soul. When we have a deep connection with a soul mate or you have just given birth to a little you, you are given overwhelming, unconditional love a gift from the universe!

We talk about *"Love"* in every aspect of our life, the word love has been used mistakenly, frivolously or even commercially, does this infringe our behaviours to this emotion? It's hard to say when I was younger I thought I was in love, but it wasn't until I meet my soul mate later in years that I realised love was a learning of diverse values, I probably did use the word love mistakenly. True love for me was a learning process. You cannot discover the true essence of you or love until it happens, how do you evaluate? Some individuals are lucky meeting their true Love at an early age and have a lifelong commitment but for other's love takes on a journey of stepping stones, a journey of connections and learning who you are as a person and what your needs are for life.

When that someone amazing steals your heart you almost know instantly that it is going to be an amazing fit. It's a corny line "you make me a better person", but especially true. The emotions you feel for a true love no words describe this connection, I've tried, but words for me don't make the grade!

Is true love achieved if you haven't learned to love and respect yourself? At certain points in time, we carry the deep burden of emotional baggage as we spoke about in forgiveness & truth. We are here on Earth to learn "its" magnificence and sometimes the unpleasant side of life and individuals. This is how we cultivate our wisdom and fortitude. But if baggage attached at your soul has you locked away it's incredibly challenging for someone to pick that lock and set you free! It has to be unlocked from within until you truly love you again you'll struggle with life's loves. You find that you have been in several relationships, but your projection of negativity becomes overwhelming for your partner and the tendency is to walk away from the relationship without any real explanation does this happen to you? Obviously not the "only" reason relationships fail. Sometimes this person just isn't your true love.

We always talk about soul mates as our true love but what if another truly distinguished soul mate said hello, the love of life! This is important for our souls. To touch the world is profound, purging life's toxins, purifying the soul and yet many of us forget about or tend to ignore nature the echo, the movement and splendour of blue skies, connecting with the oceans and rivers, walking in sync with nature, breathing nature's oxygen. We all talk about saving the world but how do we connect if our souls do not resonate with the elements of the world. Collective changes for our best soul mate planet earth transform a time of reckless behaviour, restores our true calling as the custodial guardians of life on this planet. People as a singular entity emit little energy but with millions of souls connected to bring about change achieving the *"Love"* of life is micro seconds away.

≈Love influences Truth

≈Love influences Forgiveness

HARMONY 4

"Harmony" for me peace and tranquillity come into play. Meditation springs to mind at this moment? Maybe writing about this word has ceased! Chilled!

Wouldn't it be a mammoth achievement if life lived in *"Harmony"* or let's look at a much smaller equation the community or even particular households? Meditation meltdown! Has there ever been a time when your visit to a friend's home started with a conversation in which the parents converse in the following; please ignore the kids their always causing mayhem and out of control, almost to those exact words? You cringe in the corner "dismayed" children jumping all over you! Never happened to you? Are you sure? I think you need to get out more! Is this a harmonised family or behavioural management in play (boundaries) have the parents given up on parenting or did the art of parenting ever start in the first place? We never want to constrain a child's spirit, but it goes back to "truths" talking with your child from the earliest of age discussing and practising *"boundaries"*.

Let's look at this household with the lack of boundaries, limitations and maybe other households with the same traits. Look at these children at a later stage of their development, with no boundaries are communities going to live in *"harmony"*? I think you already know the answer?

Showing you how values and words are correlated to actions through:

≈Truth creates Harmony

≈Forgiveness creates Harmony

≈Love creates Harmony

I call them mystical words, life values with the power to connect to our soul and mind. Formidable words when connected.

With the ever increasing world demands on time and living restraints *"Harmony"* is about living with our surrounds, neighbours, friends and family. In the page of *"Love"* we talk about connecting with our natural world to take time out to recharge your souls. This is Harmony! I've always had a passive disposition; harmony reflects my beliefs and values and in fact my life does not function well without balance, I'm exceedingly lucky that I have attracted a life partner with the same qualities.

We both respect each other's values and over the years grown in sync with our actions and movements. For me, I must honestly say this is *"Harmony"*.

"Harmony" for some, this practice "values" does not come easy. A life time of habits creates limitations and at first you'll need persistence to achieve this goal. City families harmonies well with long work hours, maybe the travel home, congestion from transport and public but should this be your total focus? We tend to make lunch plans within a micro second but making the simplest decision for a life change takes dedication, flexibility and sometimes the hardest step to take. The decision for change, retreat to the natural world several hours per week and recharge your soul batteries and not your laptop.

The universe is an amazing tool increase your consciousness if you just ask for *"Harmony"*

HAPPINESS 5

"Happiness" the word alone puts a smile on your face. It instantly brings up good memories and positive luminosity. Euphoric with laughter! The word *"Happiness"* sways our persona our body language injects your soul with a feel good vibe.

Have you ever heard of the law of attraction; within any circle of friends we are constantly connected to certain persons, bees to a honey pot, but why? Is it because these individuals impart energy? Making us feel amazing? Both are correct; we tend to be involved and attract the same "like" minded friends and the circle glows with contentment.

Think back for a moment to your initial meeting with your current partner was it laughter or smiles that caught your attention and made you feel comfortable in their presence, or when your child is first born, and you received that awe-inspiring first smile! Immeasurable feelings and thoughts to conjure up! Are you feeling good at the moment! This is bliss at "its" best, extremely uplifting.

When you look at children, you see and feel some children give the impression they're happier in contrast to others is it because we are born with different personalities? Possibly!

Or there has been a conflict or incident in a child's life that this child is holding close to their heart? Maybe! Remember these words *"Truth"* *"Forgiveness"* *"Love"* & *"Harmony"* Are all coupled to *"Happiness"*!

≈Happiness requires Truth

≈Happiness requires Forgiveness

≈Happiness requires Love

≈Happiness requires Harmony

Can we teach *"happiness"*? Maybe teach is too strong or even wrong but we differently influence how our children view the world. We don't have to display joy all the time but without doubt it pays to laugh and smile almost all the time.

I observe teenagers with more material wealth than other generations before them. All coupled to mobile phones, text messaging, hunched back walking into walls and people, pouting because friends have not "liked" them on facebook! Pouting from being bullied on facebook! Nonstop gaming online, spending copious amounts of hours or days destroying everything in their path, or being destroyed pouting to a loss. Children pouting for days on end with the "wants" and parents reluctantly purchasing more trying to avoid conflicts!

Does this sound familiar to you? Isn't it time to communicate your feelings *"Truth's"* it's never too late to introduce boundaries *"Harmony"* Influence a family change in direction *"Love"* Forgive yourself *"Forgiveness"* Money does not buy *"Happiness"*.

My views are more concurrent to the universe providing me with answers to my questions but of recent times science has given us the technical answers to why we feel good when we laugh, we release endorphins the feel good hormones. The grandeur of this science, laughter, is free. Drug companies can't package this virtue in any jars and place warning labels. The side effects are outrageous; please give me more side effects! My belief to this outrageous virtue *"happiness"* influences our persona, our soul, doctors are just starting to use laughter in hospitals to speed up and assist with the healing process. It's amazing the universe has given the human race this ability to be profoundly happy since the beginning of time and science is just coming to terms of late, understanding the power of this magnificent virtue *"happiness"*.

GIVING 6

"Giving" the greatest gift of all, Life! When we are born to this universe, we have received the gift of life. How we utilise this gift is up to our parents to create the first steps of learning and for us to continue this journey and gain positive growth with every aspect of life. Nearly all individuals have numerous challenges throughout life, contribute to your challenges, strength with persona, correct choices, learn from the experience and not take it as a universal judgement. As we progress through our teenage years, we are starting to focus on life out of school seeking entry to the work force. I always hear parents say the same thing to their children. "You are able to do anything you want to in life". Where is the Truth in this statement? I have to ask is this the reality? Or are you setting your child up for failure? All our children are born with certain attributes & gifts. All children attain individual goals and achievements in their life time. Shouldn't the statement be whatever paths you have chosen make sure you give 110% commitment to your life practices, after all isn't their life a Gift.

If life is a gift why do children have such a materialistic view of the world? Want! Want! Want! How do children start to take responsibility for their own actions if we are the generation that has allowed and fashioned the generation of greed. For some families, our children have left the nest but are still wanting from their parents. The wanting never stops until we as parents talk about *"Truth's"* boundaries. Discuss with our children "Forgiveness" for not showing them the universal way of *"Giving"* to others and maybe for some parents to explore this lesson also. Showing how *"Giving"* creates "Happiness" and how these two influential virtues connect on many levels. Owning the latest mobile phone is not happiness it is a short term fix until the next "want" comes along, a materialistic addiction with no cure. Continually buying material items to prove you love a child, is not love or giving! Love has no boundaries, no limits, why do you limit your love to a piece of plastic. How does a gift from Love be a special occasion when it is an everyday occurrence?

The gift of *"Giving"* When we give we are seeking approval for that Gift. We wait and scrutinize the face, waiting for that extraordinary smile to behold. The Gift of giving, in return it puts a smile on our face and gives *"Happiness"* the feel good approach to life.

You hear of great stories of giving. Individuals not just waiting for birthdays or especially holiday seasons to spread good will, their gift is to strangers all year round and if you ask them why? It touches their heart when you get that amazing smile. Imagine the feeling of Christmas 365 days of the year. Magical!

In our universe, we connect with all levels of giving from personal gifts to nation building. We have extraordinary individuals in our community that require no gifts, but maybe a hug, or a thank you. Their thanks are contributing to their community with their involvement. An assembly of persons that come to mind are volunteer's giving of themselves. Speaking proudly for Australian volunteers, without volunteers contributing to every aspect in our community's composition many organisations struggle to function. Maybe this gift of *"Giving"* has your name stamped on a badge? It doesn't cost anything but time; it contributes to the harmony of the community, brings about growth for you as a person and for the organisation you volunteer for. Maybe every volunteer should get a special hug every day?

The secretive side of *"Giving"* is your donations to Charities to bring about their causes. For all donations made, generally the person knowing about your donation is you.

Why does it give us the same feeling as giving a personal gift? The universe has opened the doors for assistance in needs of crises. When the community needs you at a local level or on a global scale, the underlying consciousness emerges for all persons. This responsiveness brings out the best in individuals. The world community functions on a higher awareness country borders disappear, wars & famine are no more. All material wealth vanishes and the true essence of the human race emerges. *"Giving"* is *"Harmony" "Forgiveness" "Love"* and *"Happiness"*

≈Giving embellishes Love

≈Giving embellishes Truth

≈Giving embellishes Harmony

≈Giving embellishes Forgiveness

≈Giving embellishes Happiness

LEARNING 7

"Learning" the nonstop approach to life, from the second we are conceived to our last breath and beyond. The brain's muscle requires exercise and stimulation every minute of the day, every day of the week! Without learning our reality ceases to exist. The universe has given us the ability to evolve our consciousness on many levels. Think about it, two hundred years ago individual perceptions had not developed to bring about understanding of universal values. Our awareness had not developed to the level of today's society and probably in another two hundred years towards our future someone reads my book and probably laughs at my level of understanding or the unthinkable! The world has lost intellectual growth and "Google" has to do our thinking for us! Gives this book a poor rating on "Google" search!! Never to be found again, lost in the main frame computer with trillions of other intellectual properties and information! Will paid information be our only source of knowledge for the future, the only source of intellect or is this fact now?

Let's ponder the second future for a split second.

Are we creating this scenario today? Do we need to exist as a society? Every question is relied upon to be answered by a computer. Technologies & computers are great I'm a fan but should we skip over our existence and go straight to the source? Do parents need to embellish wisdom on a different level connecting with the universe, bringing forth a consciousness of mystical words: *"Truth"* *"Forgiveness"* *"Love"* *"Harmony"* *"Happiness"* and *"Giving"* If we are going to let the computer do our *"learning"* then we need to reflect & resonate on a higher plane of existence & knowledge. Maybe as parents this is our future and our *"Learning"*?

≈Learning Truth's

≈Learning Forgiveness

≈Learning Love

≈Learning Harmony

≈Learning Happiness

≈Learning Giving

Our *"learning"* takes on many paths and takes us on a lifetime of journeys good and indifferent. How we learn from our actions determines who we are, our substance, fortitude and resilience. People's natures are amazing to observe.

Thought provoking when a person has just come out of an indifferent incident some individuals still repeat the same cycle of learning later in life knowing that it is still going to be a negative experience, but continue on that same path repeatedly throughout their life! You hear this continually in relationships, individuals attracting the same style of a person knowing that it is going to be a caustic connection. Why? Life is a habit forming; we get up, go to work, come home and make the same connections with individuals and therefore you need to break the habit! Take the time out, learn the universal approach, ask the universe for what you want in a person, what you want for your life and write non materialistic goals. Create a mystical practise that changes your conscious level of thought. Create your new future and not the cycle of attraction.

You also see the other side of the coin where individuals have attracted a negative experience in their life. Learned from the experience and determined never to repeat that same path again. My beliefs are some souls are born with higher consciousness of *"learning"* but it takes no time to awaken these attributes. We are all born with these skills, to active these gifts parents teach us at an early stage of development and for some children they go on many journeys to realise their *"learning"* needs to change.

FRIENDSHIP 8

"Friendship" my persona thrives with friendship. Throughout your life, you'll attract a handful of extremely good friendships, lifelong friendships. Other individuals resonate with your connection here for life's micro second and gone the next, adding to the flavour of life. Friendships elevate your inner being no "pouts" or "grunts" when we connect with friends we communicate, laugh at life's hurdles and make fun of ourselves. We are in a relaxed mood, able to change the world at a moment's notice. Differently after a few more wines! I couldn't imagine life not connected to friendship, society and the community. Nearly all my professions have involved the public in some way or another, wonderful journeys of *"friendships"*.

I've been blessed from birth; I had an extremely good upbringing. My parents taught me life values; their values fashioned who I am today. *"Love" "Forgiveness" Truth's" "Giving" "Harmony" "happiness" "friendship"* I knew when I over-stepped my boundaries this is all part of growth, but it's how my parents resolved my learning, guidance, understanding and using seven values to develop my childhood.

At an early age, I was lucky to be introduced to my parent's friends. I knew it was a privilege to be sitting in the presence of adults. Learning manners and boundaries were the key to be given these privileges again. I have to ask the question is that parenting of friendship? I think both.

Being a parent or friend to your child the great divide? Is this every parent's trepidation? Do you need to be both? Is there a fine line or do you need to combine both practices. It's irresponsible just to be a friend to your child. How do children learn the rights or wrongs that are sociably accepted in our current society or community? How are children going to learn boundaries? Manners are socially accepted throughout all languages globally even if you can't speak the language, please and thank you is an ice breaker to communicate body language, a smile. This basic skill-set enhances our opportunities, removes barriers not just with other languages but within our life's journey. As a friend do you teach your child this skill set or does a parent contribute to the education? Possibly we have too many friends providing our child's basic skill sets. You have to ask yourself does a parent set their child up for failure or their friend.

Your child's journey is going to be demanding at best with lots of curve balls to duck and weave. You keep telling us your little friend is capable of doing "anything" when your child matures? Maybe the parent needs to request an answer from the universe and not the friend, advisable to use these three words though: Please & Thank You.

≈Friendship relies on Truth

≈Friendship relies on Love

≈Friendship relies on Forgiveness

≈Friendship relies on Giving

≈Friendship relies on Harmony

≈Friendship relies on Happiness

≈Friendship relies on Learning

AFFECTION 9

"Affection" is this the connection for souls, an underlying energy in play here? We all love affection from birth to our last breath. We bond through intimacy and touch, stimulates affection, a silent bondage for partners, family and friends closest to you. My last tender moment with my Dad just before he passed away, he gave me a kiss on the cheek and had not done that for many years. Just writing about this brings back the memories and that moment. Nearly all parents that lived the war years it was hard to show affection it just wasn't done. Hard for someone to break a life time of habits but it says to me that we don't realise how time vanishes in a blink and we should all remind ourselves to not fear as fathers the astonishing power of *"Affection"*.

2013 and how things have changed several generations on and parenting for men has taken on a whole new level of affection. Amazing! We are not afraid to show our feminine side, OK maybe a little! "Only" if I get to watch the football tonight! But genuinely in today's society not showing affection to our children is frowned upon.

It seems equality is starting to happen in parenting roles, no longer is the father the bad cop and the mother the good cop, both parents are taking responsibility to providing a good grounding for their children and affection from both parents is the way to go. At the same time, it's important that your children learn this great gift *"Affection"* is a two way street and needs to be taught without prompting or bribery to give a hug in return.

If you said to me, I didn't need affection! I'd be questioning what went wrong? Looking for a thousand cures scurrying around in my head, thank you "Google"

I'd want to fix you with an embrace, but that's right you don't need affection. My first and last resort I'd have to appeal to these mystical words for an answer? *"Truths" "Forgiveness" "Love" "Giving" "Harmony" "Happiness" "Friendship"* Was the lack of intimacy with these words in childhood responsible, possibly? Has there been an indifferent event to cause this barrier, maybe? Were you born without any emotions, I have to question that? Is it possible for a person to remove the blockage to affection? Without a doubt, you have to search for that event or events that have formulated the barrier. It takes a stronger you to reach out for help or a strong partner to melt the barrier to non existence.

But when you reach for that bottle of *"Affection"* and unscrew the lid a whole new universe is ready to say hello.

≈Affection involves Love

≈Affection involves Giving

≈Affection involves Harmony

≈Affection involves Happiness

≈Affection involves Friendship

≈Affection involves Learning

≈Affection involves Truth's

≈Affection involves Forgiveness

RESPECT

"Respect" many individuals in my life I respect and value. When we are influenced by someone's positive attributes, goodwill or intellect we value those traits. When we favour someone from respect, we tend to emulate those values. It stimulates growth for a healthier approach and intellectual understanding we excel with this new level of reverence and mingle our conscious learning with others. Your circle of friends seems to attract like-minded people.

Can your child have *"Respect"*? Does your child respect your role as a parent and your life values or are you taken for granted? Is there an expectation you'll do everything for your children and your children are happy to reoccupy their seat in front of the computer or television, grunting occasionally with command? Do you say to yourself my child has this attitude where does it come from? Here's the kicker, and you won't agree with this but it comes from you and you're not alone! We have created several generations now with expectations you'll do everything for them. The "want" mentality for some reason we have compensated love for material items and this give me approach.

Buy a quick fix or it's easier and quicker for me to do the chore? Does this sound familiar? Someone you know? Is there a better way to gain respect? The first step parents have to give away the usual excuse I'm time poor with work and home commitments it easier and quicker for me to do it. Stop compensating for the lack of your child's *"Respect"*!

Let's talk a simpler option, is it time to sit down and start speaking the *"Truth"* It's never too late to discuss boundaries, communicate feelings and your expectations to start forming first class life habits instead of bad. But best of all start teaching your child life skills and if a chore takes an extra 10 minutes so be it, practiced learning brings out the best in people.

Children can't value what you do unless your children do it on a recurring basis themselves. I see much youth that can't cook the basics because mum does it all for them. How are teenagers going to give respect to their future partners progressing onto their next stage in life? Does the cycle continue? Then you are wondering why the grand children are inheriting your child's traits. Heard this story before?

Teaching life skills to your children starts life foundations where children understand *"Respect"* you and your role within the household and as a parent.

Bear in mind this young generation has more education and smarts than any generation before them. Don't let grunting or a pout fool you? Next time your child grunts or pouts give it back and laugh! Your child soon learns to change their ways. Before a child *"Respects"* your values, you have to communicate and teach the value of *"Respect"*. Love conquers all.

≈Respect in Love ≈Respect in Happiness

≈Respect in Giving ≈Respect in Friendship

≈Respect in Truths ≈Respect in Learning

≈Respect in Forgiveness ≈Respect in Affection

≈Respect in Harmony

PERSISTENCE 11

"Persistence" the purist word without doubt. Maybe science has an explanation for the energy behind this value but I can't put it into words. Does our existence correlate to who we are without persistence? It's what pushes us to be a better person, gain intellect and communicate at a higher consciousness. Grand achievements have been created with this energy it breaks all barriers to achieve goals. When we use persistence, magical qualities appear. Dream big with persistence and reality is created!

So how does *"Persistence"* fit your life? Do you class yourself as the Hare or the Turtle obviously the Hare is slightly quicker but are these two factors really significant? We still need persistence to get the job complete, without persistence no individual finishes at all. A pure principle, it not the speed that wins it's how we all cross the winning line!

Sport is the perfect analogy for *"Persistence"*, although there has to be a winner in sports. *"Persistence"* pushes everyone to be that winner. Determined in their approach to get the win!

Sports seem to come natural for a few, for others lots of practice is needed to make individuals gritty, that time we spend pushing ourselves to be a better player determines how we view the win. Some individuals are happy to surpass their last performance and for others it has to be a straight out win. In sport or life perceptions of how we commit to the game or life influence your viewpoints and attitude.

As we all grasp new skills through childhood persistence plays a big part to our persona. *"Persistence"* drives our first steps without persistence, imagine not being able to walk I'm having a visual right now of everyone sliding around on their backsides, not pretty!

Analogous in Sport are comparable to life without that practice and determination to get up every time we fall over a life wouldn't happen. Persistence is the essence that drives the human race to make a better you.

How do we extract our best qualities from childhood? As we all know, practise is sometimes boring and tedious at best. But if we start to include these potent values in the mix it changes a child's perception. *"Truth" "Love" "Forgiveness" "Giving" "Harmony" "Happiness" "Friendship" "Affection"*

It's not the gold or silver medal that should be rewarded it should be the *"Persistence"* that got them there. Not every child is going to get an "A" but if your children cross the winning line *"Persistent"* to do better that's your gold.

≈Persistence in Truth

≈Persistence in Love

≈Persistence in Forgiveness

≈Persistence in Giving

≈Persistence in Harmony

≈Persistence in Happiness

≈Persistence in Friendship

≈Persistence in Affection

≈Persistence in Respect

≈Persistence in Learning

DREAM 12

"Dream" dreaming and being does our dreaming define who we are? Is there a different silhouette of consciousness that characterises our individualism? We all have the ability to dream big, dreaming opens the door for our creativity it's responsible for our majestic intelligence it is infinite with no faults, it involves no human touch or confined with boundaries. Some of our greatest worldly achievements derived from dreams. If we did not dream how do we define tomorrow's existence? Does our life become an impasse and creativity stops?

When a baby is born you wonder what their dreams involve, as parents we know it is happening but how and what? We have not shown them speech or play maybe intelligence and dreams are predestined at conception creating our individualism and fashioning our path of life. Is this universal law creating our individual journeys of discovery and learning, the source for our reasoning and intellect? Let's contribute to our child's dreaming with "values" and not abstract points of view.Keep their dreams pure of thought.

What if a stumbling block took hold of your child's development and shatters your child's dream? If life is predestined, in our dreams do we have the freedom to dream of a greater life, bigger and better to overcome this earthly weight or do we dream a cycle of scrutiny and withdrawal. Both are predetermined by our own disposition.

As we learn, we know when we have done wrong it plays on our minds and we dream of correcting this wrong doing over and over until our conscious is clear. Part of a child's learning process is dreams. Children dream to be infinite, kicking the ball over and over scoring goals. Emulating their sporting hero or valued friend's sparks reality and achieving this dream in real life. But if their dream is shattered children tend to hide the ball and give up on ever kicking a goal. Your influence over your child's development does create sweet dreams or a cycle of vandalism. Try not to graffiti a child's dream it takes many coats of paint to recover their life qualities & individualism.

How far does a dream take you? Dream interpretation every dream has a meaning and a subconscious purpose. I have yet to discover the answers, but I do love to dream. Without my dream, this book does not exist.

Saying Gary George "author" sounds oblique!

Writing has taken me on a new journey of discovery a new dream. I asked the universe for assistance to bring my dream to reality. In my dream I awaken parent's, family and friends to values in actions and words spoken with their children, mindful to how we view the world without *"truths"* My gift to you is to awaken your life values your gift to me is to uphold these values and continue to follow your *"Dream"*

≈Dream Truths

≈Dream Love

≈Dream Forgiveness

≈Dream Giving

≈Dream Harmony

≈Dream Happiness

≈Dream Friendship

≈Dream Learning

≈Dream Affection

≈Dream Respect

≈Dream Persistence

VALUES 13

"Values" what *"Values"* resonate with you? Is it your latest mobile phone purchase or the smile on your child's face? Honestly! I have to text you back later! Did you take a bit too long to answer that question? With optimism, it was a smile on your child's face. We forget the simple properties of life that create who we are. Without the trees outside do we breathe oxygen? Isn't *"Life"* the greatest value, planting more trees to breathe or to buy more timber furniture? Your choice do *"wants"* reverberate in your life and override an honest approach to life. This question is yours to answer?

"Values" are intoxicating but simplistic in nature. Does a community exist without values? It probably does, but you wouldn't want to live there! No morality, justice, honesty, courtesy or harmony. It wouldn't be my choice to live this life style, but individuals create false values and do. Does this style of community or friendship taint your child's environment? What values do you see missing in your children's actions? As parents should we try to resolve our child's *"Values"*? No child should learn the negatives of life and *"False values"*

Do we really understand and appreciate the value of *"Life"*, I'm not a tree hugger, but I understand that we connect and echo with the world on many levels. We learn about Mathematics, English and Science etc. but have we misplaced the biggest education of all *"Life"*? Our purpose on life is not to *"want"*, but to *"give"*. With *"want"* this creates greed we are never satisfied; it resembles the dragon's breath burning everything in "its" path, manipulating everyone to get "its" way, viewing the world with blinkers on and the focus is itself.

Do you smile or are you the "grunter" or "pouter"? If we had a choice, no person wants to live with these two traits! We all know eventually the dragon's breath takes aim and scalds us!

"Giving" the higher resonance and *"Wanting"* the malicious virtue. Amazing how two words are polar opposites, both have the same fortitude. Deciding to take the path to *"Give"* when we give it does not have to be a gift. Giving a helping hand to your family, friends or community is almost the supreme value of all. Your soul flutters with undulation a quick fix for your celestial health and the community around you flourishes. Look at the Queensland floods and how over "one hundred thousand" individuals from the community volunteered to help strangers to clean up the debris.

The power of *"Give"* What *"Values"* do you encourage for your child?

A smile is *"Giving"* maybe you were born to smile, or your parents created this life time habit either way it is a gift that you should never lose. Individuals are drawn to this connection it crafts you a lifetime journey of unstoppable pathways. If you enhanced the value of *"Giving"* with the value of *"Politeness"*, it's a winning combination. The influences of these *"Values"* are unmeasurable, gifts from the universe. *"Values"*

≈The value of Truth

≈The value of Respect

≈The value of Persistence

≈The value of Learning

≈The value of Dream

≈The value of Love

≈The value of Forgiveness

≈The value of Giving

≈The value of Harmony

≈The value of Happiness

≈The value of Friendship

≈The value of Affection

ENCOURAGE 14

"Encourage" what encourages you to take your first steps in the morning. Is life habit forming? Get up go to school go to work the same habitual routine Monday to Friday and even when we are retired we tend to be still locked into this routine and frown! Shouldn't you "Encourage" yourself to break the habit? We tend to do this when we are on holidays, every day is a new adventure and for some reason our first steps in the morning are taken with leaps and bounds. A surge of internal energy, our persona, grows a 1000%.

The routine of life is it encoded in our DNA or can we reprogram our life? I think both. Do we need to encourage ourselves to reshape life's habitual routines. We still need to go to school or work six to eight hours a day but couldn't there be a mix in the other sixteen hours of the day. Does the news need to come on precisely at six or do we all need to step away from this routine and try something new. Scary stuff! Does it need to be a weekend to invite a friend for dinner? "Giving" connect with a laugh "Happiness" discuss "Truths" are we talking holiday mode now! Explore options to change a lifetime of habits.

Even if you did lift your persona 100% every day wouldn't that *"Encourage"* you to be a better person!

From the birth, we are encouraged to process life's journey of learning on a daily basis. Every second seems a life time. Life has not started "its" habitual habits yet. Every day is a holiday and our expansion of the world is growing exponentially with every lesson. We are in aura with every hug a kiss, we glow with affection. We speak several languages because we have not perfected our own. We are food critics with no understanding of the elements.

We dream of a new amusement park each day; creativity has no boundaries. Life is simplicity, uncomplicated by material wealth and items. A child's holiday is encouraged every day, maybe we need to join the *"Journey"* to continue this beautiful, uncomplicated pathway later in life. The universe has created this simplicity to *"Encourage"* the true appreciation of life.

If there were an element in life that encouraged us to be a better person how do you describe it? What name do we give it? How do you bottle this element? I think it is impossible to say that a singular element is responsible for our journey. To create a better person we need a mishmash of *"values"*, after reading all twenty five values, your awakening are these words.

Even awakening a singular value for your soul, this value encourages you to implement the smallest of change. This journey was worth taking for a better you.

On our journey do individuals *"Encourage"* harmful or constructive behaviour? Depending on your life lessons and where your values sit on the universal scale? Individuals manipulate their connections with people. Some individuals are easily manoeuvred or corrupted to think negative options have merit until this individual gets caught, or corrects the error of their ways. Classic example is civil wars, leaders persuading members of society to engage with war to empower a few. Leaders and followers play roles in our journey. Individuals influence in a positive or negative. Our *"choices"* at school work or play determine our interaction. If we stripped away the layers of moral fibre do we find the reality that material wealth, money plays a large part of someone's self image, continually seeking or gloating about money and material wealth, stomping over society to place their order! The universe request and *"Encourages"* them to review their life practises and make a choice to change.

ENCOURAGE 14

≈Encourage Truth

≈Encourage Love

≈Encourage Forgiveness

≈Encourage Giving

≈Encourage Harmony

≈Encourage Happiness

≈Encourage Friendship

≈Encourage Affection

≈Encourage Respect

≈Encourage Persistence

≈Encourage Learning

≈Encourage Dreams

≈Encourage Values

GOALS 15

"Goals" a sense of accomplishment "triumph" you have attained your goal! A pat on the back, the gold star for your achievements, this value drives us as an individual or a collective. Society and personal *"Goals"* and "Persistence" drive our existence! Are there new town centres, freeways, tunnels and sky scrapers to name a few and do we have the skills to build these visions?

Without *"Goals"* how do we achieve, how do we strive to cross the winning line! You hear of many individuals, not setting goals and wondering why your life journey is, floundering. *"Goals"* live in our future. Setting your *"Goals"*, reminding you constantly what steps are needed to bring these objectives to reality. This life practice of reaching and accomplishing brings growth and stirs your soul when you have attained your *"Goal"*.

Before you booked a holiday in a foreign country generally, some planning comes first? Researching flights, sightseeing tours and general etiquette's for the country before you pay? *"Goals"* are no different if we book a vacation in a blink of an eye surely booking several *"Goals"* are much easier, look at the journey that gets you there and arrive at your destination.

Top level athletes, business individuals use short and long term goal setting, implementing motivation and a plan on how to achieve. This formula "winning" creates gold. I'm sure we have all heard of the term bucket list? Something says to me these goals are long term.

Make you goals sharp, clearly defined. Goals aren't about winning the Lottery. Remember the "wants" in life as discussed with other values. Focus your *"Goals"* to realistic ventures or "needs".

Sometimes goals won't always be reached, but it gives us something to aim for, it makes us better & stronger individuals for trying. Great accomplishments achieved start with small steps. Start small encourage colossal.

A great quote from Thomas Jefferson

"Nothing stops the person with the right mental attitude from achieving their goal; nothing on earth helps the person with the wrong mental attitude".

When you look at the influence of *"Goals"* every aspect of life reverberates with the decision to contribute to goals, their connection to all the other values influences your future.

Your own introduction to this book and signing an undertaking to do better for your child and you, is that not a *"Goal"*? Think about the steps you need to achieve for the greatest goal of all, Your Child's *"Goals"*.

≈Set goals for Truth

≈Set goals for Love

≈Set goals for Forgiveness

≈Set goals for Giving

≈Set goals for Harmony

≈Set goals for Happiness

≈Set goals for Friendship

≈Set goals for Affection

≈Set goals for Respect

≈Set goals for Persistence

≈Set goals for Learning

≈Set goals to Dream

≈Set goals for Values

≈Set goals to Encourage

SHARING 16

"Sharing" perceptions of a child, when I was a small child I have to say I had trouble sharing. Not food or the simple things but probably my personal toys. I always had respect and looked after my toys treated them with huge kindness. I cherished a gift because it was not every day you received a gift. Whereas my brother, long term toys for him was six weeks, somehow his toys fell to pieces not the perception I wanted for my toys. My toys weren't daily occurrences. We certainly were not a rich family quite the opposite when I received a gift *"Sharing"* was unthinkable, the possibility of breaking in six weeks unforgiving! As a child, it took me several years to learn that toys were inert objects and more enjoyment came from playing with my brother then worrying about how the toys were going to be looked after. My parents persisted with this and dissolved the beginnings of a life time bad habit. I still cherish and respect my items, but family always comes first.

My parents shared everything providing food for us even at their expense going without. Sharing the value of life and respect, how to laugh even when times are tough, and money the old saying "money doesn't grow on trees" and foremost love lots of love. Love was free. I think when the family is poor everything becomes astonishing you never take anything for granted. You respect every aspect of your life; this gives you a great grounding for when money starts to flow. Life after poverty still has value. A parent from the fifties & sixties their union was family friends learning to share from no choice. Sometimes you had to borrow from your family and friends, and the favour was returned in kindness. This family connection happened daily families knew no different. *"Sharing"* was a part of life.

Move to 2013, not knowing or not wanting to know our neighbours. How perceptions have changed us, we live in insulated and isolated worlds our focus has become "likes" on "facebook" an appalling contact with our community except through restaurants, complaining there's no free internet connection or the meal is not ready in five minutes! Our selfish behaviour is creating generations with non social-able skills. It's all about me! And how we take but never give back. *"Sharing"* some western societies still rely heavily on the mature generations to instigate a sharing process. Our social skills do not rely on text messaging or communicating through computers it's a simple process of talking directly with family and friends avoiding unresponsive images on a computer.

What happens when our generation leaves this mortal plain? Have we shared the attributes needed to reverberate the next generation to contribute and understand their "soul" purpose or do future generations organise BBQ's at the micro wave, synthetic sausages being unwrapped for dinner? Their digital watch becomes a five centimetre movie screen don't need share? Dinner parties cease to exist! Cooking skills cease to exist. The micro-wave is "king" reality is prepared in a box with no understanding of why or how to create, drawn to a beep to eat layers of flavoured cardboard. How does a future generation share if we do not instigate the value of sharing? Maybe before future generations start to populate the world with their fabricated children and synthetic hearts, parents learn to change our children's perceptions and values of *"Sharing"*.

≈Share Truth

≈Share Love

≈Share Forgiveness

≈Share Giving

≈Share Harmony

≈Share Happiness

≈Share Friendship

≈Share Affection

≈Share Respect

≈Share Persistence

≈Share Learning

≈Share Dreams

≈Share Values

≈Share Goals

≈Share Encouragement

COMPASSION 17

"Compassion" I made a fundamental error in my haste today. An elderly gentleman was out shopping; I knew he was struggling, shuffling his feet at a snail's pace with the shopping trolley. In my haste, I walked past him. Not asking the question I should have done "do you need help"? This action would have taken less than ten seconds out of my busy schedule. Lucky for this gentleman a lady did stop to ask that question and graced a helping hand. An immediate sense of guilt came over me. I looked at this gentleman and sensed a slight gaze back, at this point feeling pretty disgusted with myself. I should have asked that same question.

It made me consider for that moment how unsympathetic we have become competing over life's schedules and at the end of the day has this impractical pace brought about a better us, or created a life with no compassion? I have to wonder, because you know what! Today I got caught hard and fast with my blinkers on. Maybe the universe passed a message onto me, today I was writing about compassion. Do we all need to reflect life's value's and start a conscious change?

We always talk about our young having no compassion but are life's speed, our persona driving the need to fit twenty four hours into eight going to create change? When we fashion this way of life for everyone, we focus on material wealth and monies creating a heartless society. If children can't learn any different, how does compassion grow? Is your attitude focused on you or how we help others in need? Maybe a 180 degree turn in our thinking or direction awakens our true selves and removes the robotic clock and blinkers attached to our soul.

What is *"Compassion"* walking in someone's shoes for a second, metaphorically speaking?

Does how we comprehend "understanding" open up our hearts, on a grand scale do we understand wars, starvation, natural disasters or do we place our blinkers on and ignore the plight of some! Someone else fixes the problem. Not enough time to answer this because you are late for the train, again! Don't forget to stampede through the crowd, step on a few toes to make the train in time and I know you'll give up your seat to help the elderly? Does your life travel this path? Maybe it's time to talk to your universe and seek change for Compassion?

"Compassion" on a smaller scale is its understanding, not every person is the same?

We all have different scales of learning, life skills and cultural diversities. Is it more compassionate to compliment learning capabilities and not criticise? When we focus on criticising personality floors in individuals through school, work, friends and the community are we cultivating their abilities or assisting to throw away the text books. Isn't it time to compliment? Is every person a bad driver or maybe we are too intolerant to look at our own driving skills? Possibly driving is a good metaphor for the real world. With a different outlook on life does your universe gain growth, remove the blinkers a few hours a day until you reach your full potential and a changed person, time to remove a life-time of robotic habits? Life is not a soap opera! It requires *"Compassion"* understanding not drama. It's time to distinguish real life from TV.

≈Compassion in Truth

≈Compassion in Love

≈Compassion in Giving

≈Compassion in Harmony

≈Compassion in Happiness

≈Compassion in Friendship

≈Compassion in Affection

≈Compassion in Respect

≈Compassion in Persistence

≈Compassion in Learning

≈Compassion in Dreams

≈Compassion in Values

≈Compassion in Goals

≈Compassion in Sharing

CELEBRATING

"Celebrating" we tend to celebrate milestones in our life, Christenings, Birthdays and significant religious occasions. But is there an immeasurable celebration we have missed? The universal gift of everyday life! Shouldn't this be our celebration? We wouldn't need to party with the same overzealous approach as we do with Birthdays but with values. Focus on our values our interaction with society, family & friends. Universal virtues are yours to choose and pick how you connect these values in your life. Celebrate to give.

The universe does not want for material gifts, but a smile a thank you! Speak to your universe. Discover what contributions awaken your journey your universe and see how the universe encourages the celebration of your life. Excommunicating your heart from the world and living the life of a solitary person achieves limited bliss; open your heart to a lifelong holiday celebration every day.

When we touch someone's heart in a good way, it's the supreme gift to us. For that expressive split second in time, you have etched a memory that stays with a person for eternity and perpetuates an inner glow for you. If we had wings, for that split second we'd soar.

My spiritual views won't connect with everyone and for that matter I don't want them to. These virtues are mine to enjoy my desired connection with the universe. Your universal path is yours to create. My beliefs do not impinge or restrict a person's outlook on life. There are no limitations for my life it can't be contained in text or beliefs, restricted to religion. My universe celebrates our mortal being, the free spirit of life.

If we released the magnificence of love does it wrap the world in bliss with open hands? Refurbish shattered souls and mend wounds. Creates harmony for communities and leaves the world with an abundance of truth, friendship, learning and respect. Learn by heart, never restrict your love of life or people, actions resonate louder than words. Celebrate love daily! Join the revolution, no guns, no violence, *"Compassion"* and *"Harmony"* My dreams! My beliefs! My revolution!

Writing this book how and why is a mystery in itself. I asked the universe: how do I assist to help children, simple question? I asked this question many times. The book was the universal answer. I've celebrated every page written. I wanted to awaken emotions with these twenty five mystical words to adapt a change in someone's life practice for the better.

The quandary, I need my beliefs to write this book, but I don't want to push my beliefs onto others. My celebration is for you to connect on a different level of understanding, enlighten how virtues make connections and influence your behaviour, sometimes not realising how trapped we have become in our daily life routine. *"Celebrating"* the change to how we connect with our children.

≈Celebrate Truth

≈Celebrate Love

≈Celebrate Harmony

≈Celebrate Happiness

≈Celebrate Friendship

≈Celebrate Affection

≈Celebrate Respect

≈Celebrate Persistence

≈Celebrate Learning

≈Celebrate Dreams

≈Celebrate Values

≈Celebrate Encouragement

≈Celebrate Goals

≈Celebrate Sharing

≈Celebrate Compassion

INSPIRATIONAL 19

"Inspirational" many inspirations in your life's journey, as children we are all inspired by parents! The greatest stimulus any child receives. Children watch mystified by their parent's actions, mimic every move, every word their individualism is being shaped by their parent's values. Their journey speaks the parent's universal path. Good or indifferent Children discover and embellish these qualities. Life's greatest inspiration is a journey mapped in love!

As we educate with ideals and worldly classes, we develop our own personal viewpoints and stance in the world. Our persona is growing at an astonishing pace, beyond our parents expectations. We still take guidance reluctantly from our parents because as you recognise "we know best". Our friends become the new teachers because "we know best". It's inspiring to watch teenager's quickness! Learning independence obviously with Mum and Dad still paying! Clever! Wanting all the worldly possessions if Mum and Dad still pay! Clever! But the good aspect about this stage in the development is the quickening of understanding and the universe opening up many new doors and inspirations.

Your football team has been deleted and chosen their own. Food takes on a new meaning exploring new cuisines and taste as a small child point blank refusing to eat. Their music choice does not resonate with yours, but it is their deafness to make.

Insightful the world is not as big as first thought and setting goals to explore every inch, surely if Mum and Dad still pay? Clever! First day of work is inspiring new steps into an endless journey of learning.

The reality of rigorous life habits has started life boundaries just stepped up a notch; restrictions on time our constant travel and work commitments hits home and the realisation that life with Mum & Dad isn't that bad after all! Thinking about staying a few more years if mum & dad still pay! *"Inspirational"*.

The biggest impact in life is family and friends meeting persons of inspiration for your life journey or your love allowing them to engage the soul. Their virtues contribute how you socially interact and your behaviours. Is this person right for your universe, does this person impact in a positive or is the connection going to be many lessons of indifference. Negative virtues are chosen? Do we learn by never making the same choice twice or avoiding the juncture in the first place?

Life is learning it's not bad to make mistakes by choice we all do, it's how we turn a lesson into a positive that's *"Inspirational"*.

Optimistically our contact with family and friends are for a lifetime, what choices do you make to be *"Inspirational"* to others? Is it the way you communicate? Do we focus on all the negatives in life or the positives? Is the glass half empty of half full? Choices in conversation attract or detract people. Is it more inspirational to listen and learn life's journey or brag about life's journey "give or receive". Every morning do we start with leaps and bounds or a pout, your choices in life? To learn the art of being inspirational, not everyone needs to be a leader it's how modest we are when we cross the finishing line that is inspirational. Cultivate inspiration and society follows in your footsteps. A lesson needed for all humanity.

≈Inspiration in Truth	≈Inspiration in Persistence
≈Inspiration in Love	≈Inspiration in Learning
≈Inspiration in Forgiveness	≈Inspiration in Values
≈Inspiration in Giving	≈Inspiration in Compassion
≈Inspiration in Harmony	≈Inspiration in Goals
≈Inspiration in Happiness	≈Inspiration in Sharing
≈Inspiration in Respect	≈Inspiration in Dreams
≈Inspiration in Affection	≈Inspiration in Celebrations

FAMILY 20

"Family" the word family does it create anxiety or a sense of warmth when we mention this word. What emotions are you feeling at this moment? How do you perceive your immediate family? Is the old saying, "you can choose your friends, but you can't choose your family" foremost in your thoughts or the opposite deep respect and love?

When we listen to individual perceptions for parents and siblings, the discussions focus on apprehension or praise with slight middle ground for both perceptions. We assume the strongest bond is family that life connection from birth and yet we see many fractured memories and hurts. Have you ever discussed *"truths"* respectfully never spoken in anger to how we feel? Understood your parent's ideals & persona or asked the question why?

With the stress, your family never knows your sadness the discussion has never happened. To bring about understanding lifting your soul to forge *"forgiveness"* or have perceptions created intimidating memories and burying *"truths"* become your universal focus? It's never too late to discuss a new way of thinking and shatter hidden *"truths"*.

If family life is perfect in every way you are the luckiest person on the planet, you won't need to buy a lottery ticket you have already won, this precious gift is imprinted on your soul forever. Discussions exploit *"happiness" "respect" "love"* and *"forgiveness"* enriching your children's children as life's endeavours continue. Ideals for some parent's come naturally and for others practiced change is needed, but either way remaining focused to deliver the same results *"persistence"* achieves a family's love

The families bond, energy impenetrable to outside influences. Society's "super-glue", virtues measured with increments of love, limitless.

Time does not falter this emotion it grows in volume as the family grows. We smile at each and every generation of siblings. Our focus is family and only family we resonate with the universe and not with material attachments deterring our focus to an inclusive *"Family"*.

To measure a family's bond have we always returned the favour, the gift, hug or smile or do we have to be swayed and asked continually to be integrated with family reunions? Is it healthier memories to give the hug first and watch the smile or receive the hug and give that precious memory to your sibling? Maybe instinctively as family you share this amazing gift with spontaneity both sharing a lifelong memory of *"Family"*.

When you reflect on *"Family"* bonds, I imagine human beings are the luckiest species on the planet we get to play and influence every child born to the family. We encourage values and laughter with every generation good or indifferent. Our greatest gift is the gift of love; we speak volumes when we use love in our language. Children's responses are heightened with a continual smile. Measure your increments of love speak volumes to your child.

≈Family with Truth

≈Family with Love

≈Family with Forgiveness

≈Family with Giving

≈Family with Harmony

≈Family with Happiness

≈Family with Friendship

≈Family with Affection

≈Family with Respect

≈Family with Learning

≈Family with Dreams

≈Family with Values

≈Family with Goals

≈Family with Sharing

≈Family with Compassion

≈Family with Celebrations

≈Family with Inspiration

≈Family with Persistence

MANNERS 21

"Manners" associated with respectful boundaries, an understanding and teachings of how to greet, communicate and respect other people's interactions. Learn the art of body language, smile, knowing when to listen and then engage in expressive conversation and not talking over people. Manners dictate how we interact with the community and the world. The virtue displayed your upbringing and their tolerance to the next part of the conversation connecting new life friends from school work and play.

"Manners" are an essential skill that needs self restraint and practised beliefs. Super intelligence an IQ of two hundred deciphering life's equations, how does super intelligence convey the simplicity of manners to converse in everybody's language, do we tolerate superior intelligence lacking manners or do individuals belittle their own intelligence without manners? Every nationality has benchmarks of acceptable behaviour and etiquette's tolerated with every community. Don't be left sitting on the bench trying to learn these skills late in life, no person wants to be standing on the side-line when everyone else is playing on the field!

Are we losing the art of manners? The mobile phone is a classic example. Do we need to listen to everyone's conversation? Don't individuals realise when their swearing or loudness has touched a child let alone the rest of the public and who really cares about your indiscretions with your boyfriend or girlfriend! Do I have to stand in line and listen to the days of your dreary? Imagine a sentence without putting the word "like" in there. Heaven! Are soap operas engaging society or parents I have to ask?

The families bond, energy impenetrable to outside influences. Society's "super-glue", virtues measured with increments of love, limitless.

Time does not falter this emotion it grows in volume as the family grows. We smile at each and every generation of siblings. Our focus is family and only family we resonate with the universe and not with material attachments deterring our focus to an inclusive *"Family"*.

To measure a family's bond have we always returned the favour, the gift, hug or smile or do we have to be swayed and asked continually to be integrated with family reunions? Is it healthier memories to give the hug first and watch the smile or receive the hug and give that precious memory to your sibling? Maybe instinctively as family you share this amazing gift with spontaneity both sharing a lifelong memory of *"Family"*.

When you reflect on *"Family"* bonds, I imagine human beings are the luckiest species on the planet we get to play and influence every child born to the family.

We encourage values and laughter with every generation good or indifferent. Our greatest gift is the gift of love; we speak volumes when we use love in our language. Children's responses are heightened with a continual smile. Measure your increments of love speak volumes to your child.

≈Family with Truth

≈Family with Love

≈Family with Forgiveness

≈Family with Giving

≈Family with Harmony

≈Family with Happiness

≈Family with Friendship

≈Family with Affection

≈Family with Respect

≈Family with Learning

≈Family with Dreams

≈Family with Values

≈Family with Goals

≈Family with Sharing

≈Family with Compassion

≈Family with Celebrations

≈Family with Inspiration

≈Family with Persistence

POLITENESS 22

"Politeness" brings back great memories the corner store was my destination to buy for my mum. The owner a beautiful, considerate Italian lady always said hello and every time I used "please and thank you" for my purchase she made a comment how polite I was and put a couple of sweets in the bag. Forty five years on I have never forgotten that lady and how "please and thank you" brought me great rewards. A life skill I have been blessed with and shared throughout my life.

As parents do we inspire these life skills to bless your child's journey? Should *"Politeness"* be etiquette to open and finish a question a request or some conversations? Without these words "please and thank you" does a request become a command, are you conversing mixed messages? Do you get the best results in life or a poor response to your request? For some reason when we ask in politeness our body language changes our facial expressions have a softer approach the words fit perfectly.

We have all associated with demanding bosses, do commands win at the end of the day probably not. When bosses put half the effort into the message, we put half the energy into the task. Why should we take it any further?

But if the boss's persona was different and "please and thank you" come into play then the information is conveyed differently we have a different attitude to how we react, the job gets completed. From a demand to a request the same conversation but with an extra three formidable words "please, thank you".

A universal law connected with all languages. It breaks through barriers opens conversations with strangers, connects with our persona. *"Politeness"* is somewhat abstract across different cultures with common underlying elements to this value, almost an understanding or expectation of your culture and consideration towards others. If someone has told you, particular cultures are abrupt in their manner and all of the sudden you hear "please and thank you" you are surprised this person has taken the effort to speak your language and open the discussion with a refreshing ice breaker.

A classic example: My partner and I were on a recent trip to China, I think after catching thirty odd taxis we finally got a taxi driver that said hello and thank you in broken English he laughed when he said it, we laughed with him when he said it and with honesty this gentleman was rewarded handsomely with a large tip. That's all he knew in English but that was enough for us.

Our life seems to evolve around retail outlets for food, clothing, materialistic items you see shop attendants mannequin in their stance and response. Is it a genuine hello, thank you or programmed response, measurement of the business structure? We know straight away from body language that a person is using robotic motions. Does the shop attendant ever smile, look you in the eye or even acknowledge you are standing there, yelling out hello looking at someone else. Should the training not be with "hello" but the actual body language behind the technique of greeting and thanking? We probably spend ten times the amount of monies on food then we spend on personal items and yet our response back from these outlets is ten times less. If *"Politeness"* and *"Values"* where the true factors for your shopping excursion why haven't we all experienced the corner store approach to *"Politeness"*.

POLITNESS 22

≈Politeness in Truth

≈Politeness in Love

≈Politeness in Persistence

≈Politeness in Giving

≈Politeness in Forgiveness

≈Politeness in Harmony

≈Politeness in Affection

≈Politeness in Happiness

≈Politeness in Friendship

≈Politeness in Respect

≈Politeness in Learning

≈Politeness in Dreams

≈Politeness in Values

≈Politeness in Goals

≈Politeness in Encourage

≈Politeness in Sharing

≈Politeness in Family

≈Politeness in Compassion

≈Politeness in Manners

≈Politeness in Inspiration

≈Politeness in Celebrations

CHOICES 23

"Choices" majestic by value or extremely destructive, we all have choices! The universe has provided us with infinite options, the power or right to select from many possible alternatives. Understanding the values of *"Choices"* without parenting to model the initial learning do we chose a negative understanding? These consequences impinge a child's life development. *"Choices"* are our behavioural floors or triumphs a lifelong lesson on our actions or non actions. Right or wrong *"choices"* are a continued life lesson?

How do we learn if every choice is correct, do we need to make mistakes, so we understand when we triumph? When we have crossed moral boundaries and committed a wrong doing against society or an individual do these decisive actions bring about tough lessons of justice and judgement that brandish *"Choices"*.

Every circular moment in the day from the moment we take our first steps to our last breath the choice is yours to improve your universe. When we first wake up in the morning do we spring out of bed or cringe at today's arrival, your *"choice"*.

When you are open and ready for infinite beginnings and possibilities your determination creates a better you! We all have different universes created by ourselves.

In my universe, I'll engage in laughter a smile, great conversation, a journey of friends and family no violence, no rudeness. My universe has an optimistic view on life it seeks the truth. What's yours? What's your child's universe? Is it time to reflect and imagine a different future to set different desires, aspirations or continue on the same path? *"Choices"*

When we have to make a decision in life, and we have two options do we listen to our intuition (gut feeling) or do we sometimes sprint with the pace of a charging bull with the "want" or "craving" knowing the instant you made your *"Choice"* it was wrong. How many times do you hear the saying "I should have gone with my gut instinct"? How do we influence our decisions? Does time and wisdom change our habits, not always? Do we need to listen to our gut feelings but also put a worldly aspect behind our decision? Use our universal values to decipher the rights or wrongs and not the charging bull!

When you are faced with two options do we look at the detriments following your decision does this guide you to the best resolve. *"Choices"*

Do we have respect or have acceptance of other people's *"choices"* even if we do not agree with their decision? Their choice is learning and growth for their universe not yours. If their selection impedes on you or the community that's when you intervene, I do not agree or condone drug taking but I understand the substitute for life an individual makes. Providing their decision does not impede on my universe or the community I'll accept their resolve. Next time you re-examine a *"choice"* listen to your gut feelings check to see if it impedes on family, friends, neighbours or the community make the best alternative? It's your journey, your understanding. *"Choices"*

Does our consciousness thrive with every generation without *"Choices"*? Or our world limited in deliberation, viewing actions and judgment with restricted understanding, life values shrink? Do we learn life challenges learn the fundamentals of right or wrong with no *"Choices"*.

CHOICES

≈Choices with Truth

≈Choices with Love

≈Choices with Forgiveness

≈Choices with Giving

≈Choices with Harmony

≈Choices with Happiness

≈Choices with Respect

≈Choices with Affection

≈Choices with Learning

≈Choices with politeness

≈Choices with Persistence

≈Choices with Values

≈Choices with Goals

≈Choices with Friendship

≈Choices with Sharing

≈Choices with Compassion

≈Choices with Celebrations

≈Choices with Family

≈Choices with Inspiration

≈Choices with Manners

DEPENDABLE 24

"Dependable" strength in action does your life connections seek a *"Dependable"* you? Are you a reliable friend, worker, father or mother? What qualities are essential to become *"Dependable"* do we need to be consistent in our actions achieving similar results or a constant performance level?

If you become, a person of dependence is this not a great accomplishment? Soul connections respect you more and see you as someone ready and able to help. *"Dependable"* individuals tend not to brag about themselves are inclined to arrive first and complete the task or chore with zealous. You are organised in your actions and life, favoured by everyone. You are *"Dependable"*.

Does this virtue contribute to good leaders? When we respect and look up to leaders in business, life, family and friends are we always requiring consistency in behaviour? Where does this trait come from? Do we mould this quality or are you born with this trait, both are correct. Our parents teach these values, you make the choices required to learn the skills? Does dependability contribute to a rising star?

Every child is a rising star and at an early age you won't know all the answers but if we create consistency in a child's learning every day becomes a day of self assurance, faith in their actions and skills. Children develop qualities desired for school, work and play. Soul connections cherish their virtues.

You have to admire small business owners. If a business opportunity arose for yourself tomorrow do you need to be *"Dependable"* consistent in demure, ethics, politeness before you make the choice to purchase or start this business? Or do you focus on short cuts contributing a sloppy work routine working for someone else?

When you are the person bringing in monies do you have the fortitude of dependence to complete the work on schedule? You must be unswerving to your customer's needs and feedback good or indifferent and learn from the indifferent? As we mature within the work force, I think nearly everyone has the desire to start their own business but do you have the *"Dependable"* attributes to get the job done!

We talk about *"Dependable"* values, but our lives are extremely reliant on technology.

It stimulates and sometimes manipulates a good chunk of our day from the alarm clock starting our day to the last meal of the day and everything in between, until we finally fall asleep in front of the television.

Yet what if everyone's technology were not reliable does society get to school or work on time. Do we abandon the car in the driveway when it breaks down? Our cook-top decided it's had enough, tired of cooking your meals, not playing the game any longer!

Is this a good thing or bad? If this happens to everyone in society do we seriously have to look for a conscious change to step away from the drama of technology and redirect our energies for a simpler format of being? Or do we persist with the madness until it finally drove us to despair! Something to think about next time your fridge is not *"Dependable"*.

≈Dependable with Love
≈Dependable with Friendship
≈Dependable with Respect
≈Dependable with Giving
≈Dependable with Harmony
≈Dependable with Happiness
≈Dependable with Truth
≈Dependable with Affection
≈Dependable with Dreams
≈Dependable with Learning
≈Dependable with Persistence

≈Dependable with Values
≈Dependable with Sharing
≈Dependable with Encourage
≈Dependable with Goals
≈Dependable with Family
≈Dependable with Truth
≈Dependable with Choices
≈Dependable with Manners
≈Dependable with politeness
≈Dependable with Inspiration

JOURNEY 25

"Journey" the journey of life an amazing speculative, micro seconds of the now and the future. We talk in the now walk "in our future". Every step is a path a conscious decisions made with spontaneity or planning. Our life path is not always clear it is exceedingly rare to decide on a singular pathway. We contribute too many journeys.

The journey is not about us but how we interact and contribute to the journey. We touch hearts we break hearts. Did we choose to use our life values or flaunt the thoughtless approach to life? Your life journal is an open book to your values and choices. Does your journal enclose mystery, a detective story, good faith, love and good will, sporting achievements or all combined?

No person has a clear answer to the future but contributing values to the *"Journey"* creates pathways filled with wonderment, surrounded with soul connections, individuals resonating with your universe and you contributing to their *"Journey"*.

This amazing passage starts from conception, a learning pathway from now to eternity. What is our awakening about? Have we made the *"Journey"* about our wants and removed the focus of contributing to our life?

What do we need to do to reconfirm our life values? Is it to realign the universal laws, remove our focus for material wealth? What if we were able to take this step does our journey take on a fluid approach to life instead of worrying about the buying needs for the next must have material item!

Do our principles come from our approach to this journey? Maybe twenty five mystical words start you on a new found journey a path of learning, an introduction to values and practices for a life time of *"Love"* and *"Giving"* to find a new you and *"Awaken"* your soul and your children's *"Journey"*.

Writing this book for me has been my *"Journey"* of late. I don't read novels my mind becomes unresponsive after the first page. I have never written a short book before, what decisive action took me on this journey? For months, I was talking to the powers to be how I wanted to assist a child's path provoke thinking away from the wants in life make a change, give values back to their life. The universal answer came in this short book. I hope this book has reached out to many souls and you have enjoyed my *"Journey"*, and I have contributed to yours and your children's *"Journey"* and provoked thought for a change.

JOURNEY 25

≈Journey with Truth

≈Journey with Love

≈Journey with Forgiveness

≈Journey with Giving

≈Journey with Harmony

≈Journey with Happiness

≈Journey with Friendship

≈Journey with Affection

≈Journey with Respect

≈Journey with Persistence

≈Journey with Learning

≈Journey with Dreams

≈Journey with Values

≈Journey with Goals

≈Journey with Encourage

≈Journey with Sharing

≈Journey with Compassion

≈Journey with Inspiration

≈Journey with Family

≈Journey with Celebrations

≈Journey with Manners

≈Journey with Politeness

≈Journey with Choices

≈Journey with Truth

≈Journey with Dependence

CHANGE 26

My personal quotes for Change

≈ Plan in the "Now" walk in the "Future" Choices create a new you!

≈ Dream big with persistence and reality is created!

≈ Please and Thank You. You decide your virtues

≈Are my words intuitive with virtues or caustic by choice

≈ Remove all hidden "Truths" choose "Forgiveness" and "Understanding"

≈ Talk with modesty action life with greatness.

CHANGE 26

≈ Cultivate inspiration and society follows in your footsteps. A lesson needed for all humanity.

≈ Life isn't about the "wants" Life is about fashioning yourself to be a better you! Dance the journey of discovery!

≈ A Child's holiday is encouraged every day, maybe we need to join the "Journey".

≈ Too truly love someone you first need to truly love you again! Unlock your soul from within to find true change & happiness!